LATE INTERMEDIATE PIANO DUETS

RODGERS AND HAMMERSTEIN™

THE SOUND OF MUSIC ®

CONTENTS

2 The Sound Of Music

76 Climb Ev'ry Mountain

30 Do-Re-Mi

68 Edelweiss

46 The Lonely Goatherd

10 Maria

18 My Favorite Things

40 Sixteen Going On Seventeen

58 So Long, Farewell

Cover Designed by FRANK "FRAVER" VERLIZZO
Cover Photo Courtesy of Twentieth Century Fox Film Corporation

ISBN 0-7935-1865-2

HAL•LEONARD®
CORPORATION
7777 W. BLUEMOUND RD. P.O. BOX 13819 MILWAUKEE, WI 53213

THE SOUND OF MUSIC

SECONDO

Lyrics by OSCAR HAMMERSTEIN II
Music by RICHARD RODGERS

THE SOUND OF MUSIC

PRIMO

Lyrics by OSCAR HAMMERSTEIN II
Music by RICHARD RODGERS

Moderato

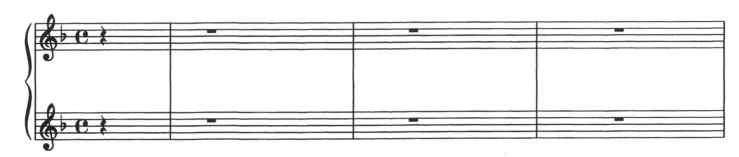

SECONDO

SECONDO

SECONDO

MARIA

SECONDO

Lyrics by OSCAR HAMMERSTEIN II
Music by RICHARD RODGERS

MARIA

PRIMO

Lyrics by OSCAR HAMMERSTEIN II
Music by RICHARD RODGERS

SECONDO

SECONDO

SECONDO

MY FAVORITE THINGS

SECONDO

Lyrics by OSCAR HAMMERSTEIN II
Music by RICHARD RODGERS

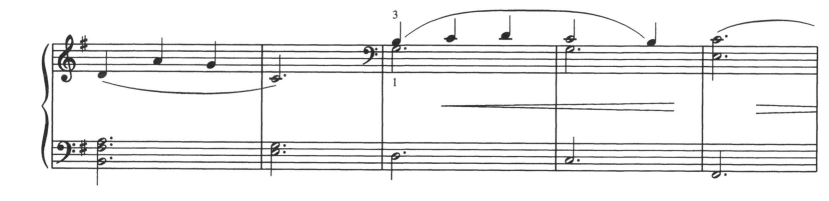

MY FAVORITE THINGS

PRIMO

Lyrics by OSCAR HAMMERSTEIN II
Music by RICHARD RODGERS

Allegro (♩. = 69)

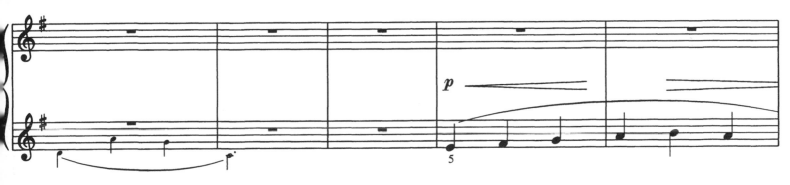

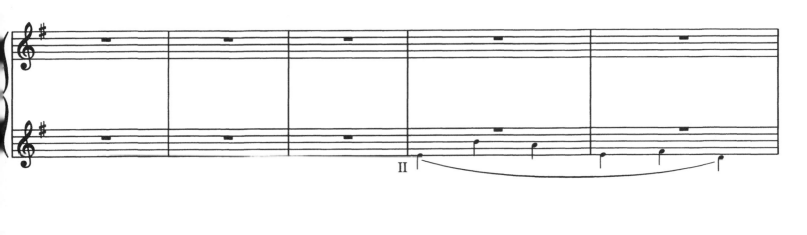

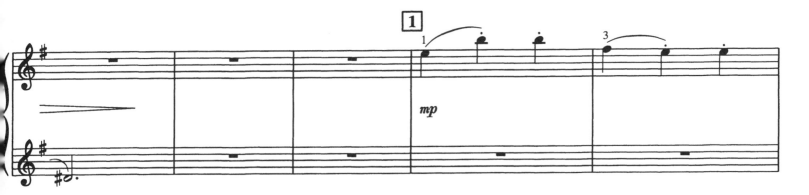

SECONDO

SECONDO

SECONDO

SECONDO

SECONDO

DO-RE-MI

SECONDO

Lyrics by OSCAR HAMMERSTEIN II
Music by RICHARD RODGERS

Allegretto

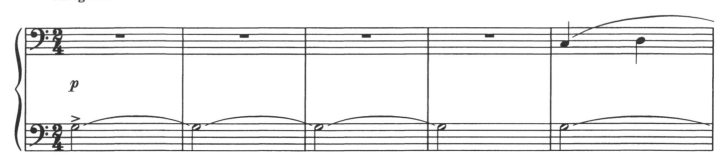

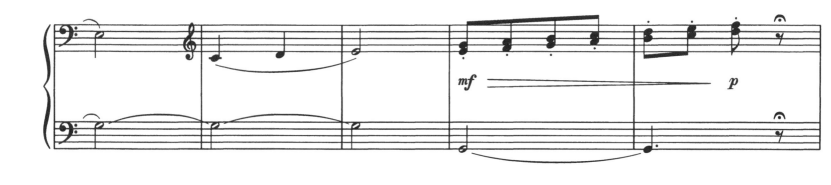

DO-RE-MI

PRIMO

Lyrics by OSCAR HAMMERSTEIN II
Music by RICHARD RODGERS

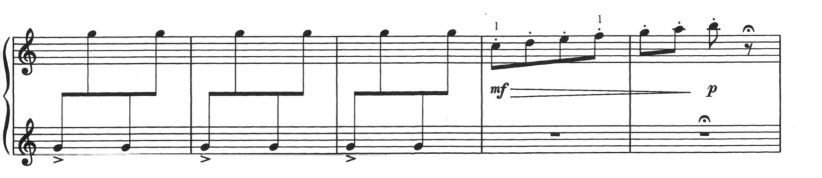

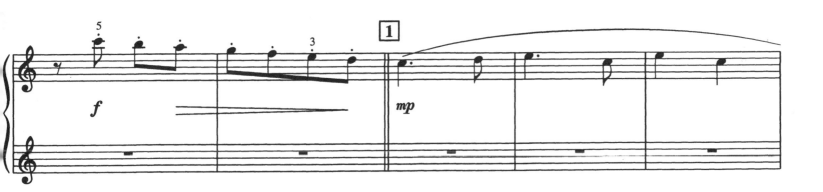

SECONDO

SECONDO

SECONDO

PRIMO

SIXTEEN GOING ON SEVENTEEN

SECONDO

Lyrics by OSCAR HAMMERSTEIN II
Music by RICHARD RODGERS

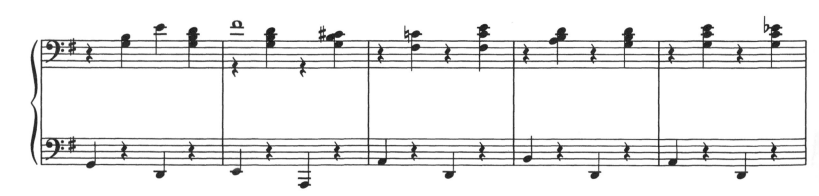

SIXTEEN GOING ON SEVENTEEN

PRIMO

Lyrics by OSCAR HAMMERSTEIN II
Music by RICHARD RODGERS

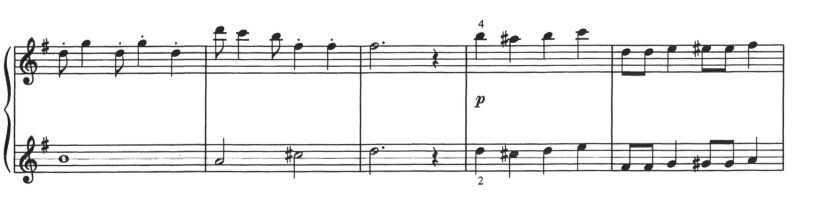

SECONDO

PRIMO

SECONDO

THE LONELY GOATHERD

SECONDO

Lyrics by OSCAR HAMMERSTEIN II
Music by RICHARD RODGERS

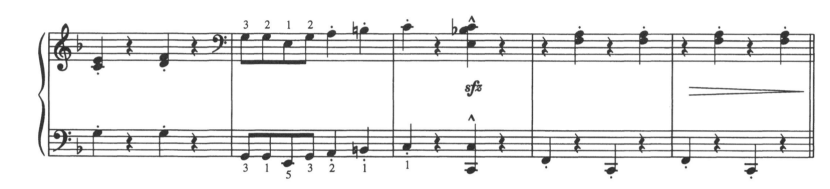

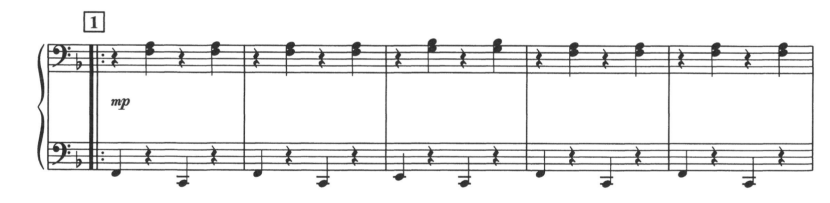

THE LONELY GOATHERD

PRIMO

Lyrics by OSCAR HAMMERSTEIN II
Music by RICHARD RODGERS

SECONDO

SECONDO

D.S. al Coda

SO LONG, FAREWELL

SECONDO

Lyrics by OSCAR HAMMERSTEIN II
Music by RICHARD RODGERS

SO LONG, FAREWELL

PRIMO

Lyrics by OSCAR HAMMERSTEIN II
Music by RICHARD RODGERS

PRIMO

EDELWEISS

SECONDO

Lyrics by OSCAR HAMMERSTEIN II
Music by RICHARD RODGERS

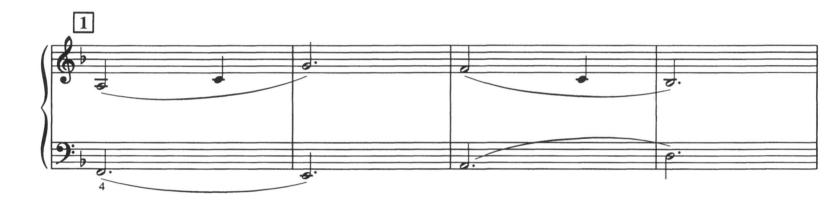

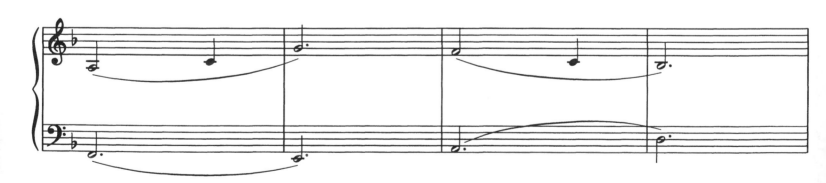

EDELWEISS

PRIMO

Lyrics by OSCAR HAMMERSTEIN II
Music by RICHARD RODGERS

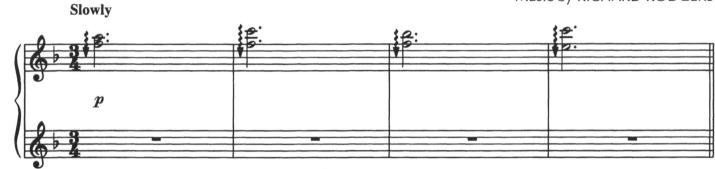

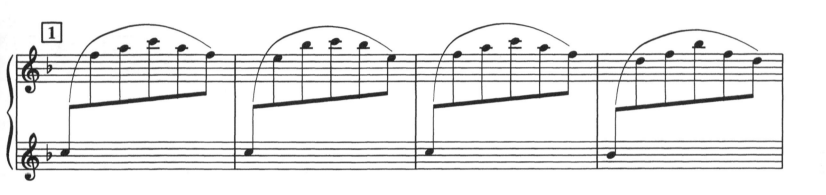

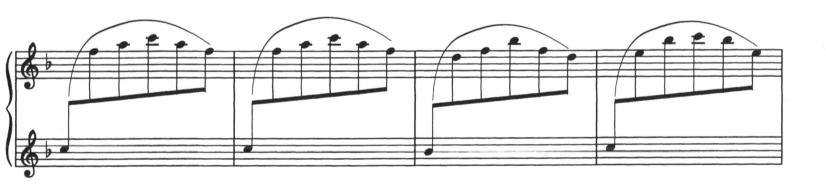

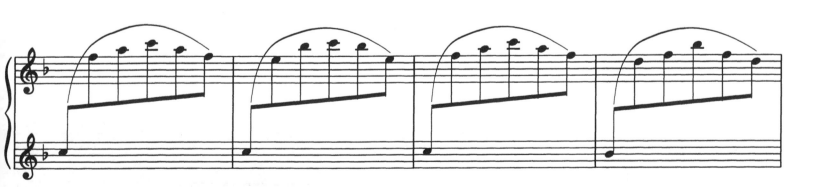

SECONDO

SECONDO

SECONDO

CLIMB EV'RY MOUNTAIN

SECONDO

Lyrics by OSCAR HAMMERSTEIN II
Music by RICHARD RODGERS

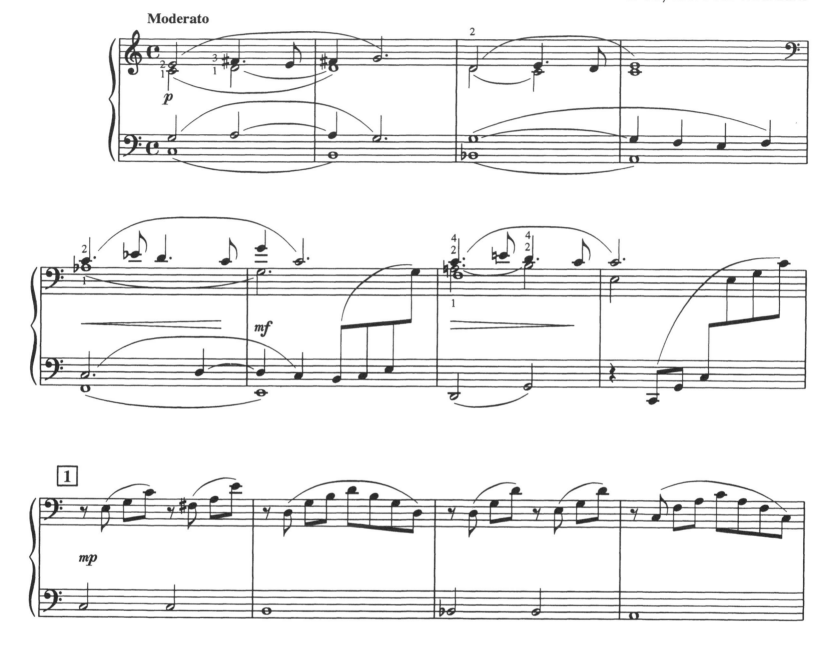

CLIMB EV'RY MOUNTAIN

PRIMO

Lyrics by OSCAR HAMMERSTEIN II
Music by RICHARD RODGERS

SECONDO